|||||||||||||||||||||||||||||
W9-ATS-919

DESIGN & FLY

PAPER
AIRPLANES

Created by the Top That! team

Copyright © 2003 Top That! Publishing plc.
Published by Tangerine Press, an imprint of Scholastic Inc.
557 Broadway, New York, NY 10012.
All rights reserved.
Scholastic and Tangerine Press and associated logos are trademarks of Scholastic Inc.
Printed and bound in China.

Getting Started

If you're crazy about airplanes, you'll love this pack. It enables you to make some amazing flying models from easy-to-create templates!

The projects are easy to do and look terrific. There are two main steps to flying high! First, choose the plane you want to build from a selection of great templates. Then personalize your fab fliers by adding color and accessories from the huge selection of each before printing them out.

From then on, every project begins with a short list of materials you'll need to continue. All you'll need to start cutting, folding, and sticking your fliers into shape is a pencil, ruler, scissors, glue, and other items you'll find around the house.

Running the CD

If you are using a PC, the program should run automatically. If not, double click on the "my computer" icon on the desktop, and then on the "CD drive" icon. Then double click on the title "art-pc.exe."

If you are using a Macintosh® double-click on the "CD" icon on the desktop, and then double click on the title "art-mac."

MINIMUM SYSTEM REQUIREMENTS

- Screen resolution 800 x 600
- CD-ROM Color depth 24-bit (true color)

PC users—Intel Pentium® 166 processor running Windows TM 95/98 or NT version 4.0 or later, 64 MB of installed RAM and a color monitor.

Macintosh® users—Power PC running System 8.1 or later, 64 MB of installed RAM and a color monitor.

Printing the templates

Before you print any of the images from the CD-ROM, check the printer settings under the "File" menu and make sure that you've

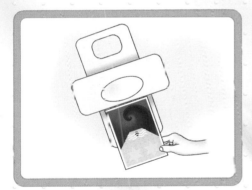

selected "quality paper." Aim to use thin but high-quality paper for the best results!

The template will fill a letter page. Check that you have selected the "Portrait" setting under the "Page Setup" menu.

Some designs require the use of scissors. Always be careful not to cut yourself or damage any surfaces—and ask an adult for help if necessary.

The User Guide

This is where all the fun begins!

Although you're probably anxious to get started, take time out to read this user guide first. It will give you lots of hints to follow to make sure that your planes look really professional. For your planes to loop the loop, keep a sharp eye out for the handy hints on each page, and follow the steps carefully!

Loading Up...

Once your CD has loaded, a Welcome Page will appear. Click onto "Enter" to go onto the next page. When you've done this, a screen will appear offering you three options. Click on "Create" and the studio will appear. This is where you put the templates together.

The Drawers

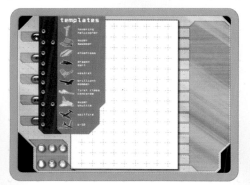

You will find five drawers on the left-hand side of the screen. They open and close with one click of the mouse. You'll build up your plane by taking parts out of each. They include basic templates and accessories with which you can personalize, or imitate, your favorite type of plane. The drawer contents will be explained later!

The Pasteboard

The pasteboard is the gray panel down the right-hand side of the screen. The parts you've taken out of each drawer appear here. To move the parts onto the main screen, close the drawer, click on the part and drag it over. You can put a maximum of 24 images onto the board. Images will overlap on the pasteboard, but click on the one you want and it will pop up.

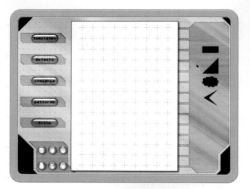

The Blank Page

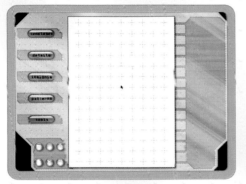

The blank page is the white rectangle with red crosses that appears in the center of the page when the studio first loads. It is the only part of the screen that will print out. Once you have chosen a template, it will fill the page, and you can start adding more parts to your plane.

What's What?

The icons at the bottom left-hand corner of the screen are short cuts that leave you more time to be creative! Here's what they all mean...

Home — Click on the "home" icon to return to the main menu. (You also need to do this to "escape" the program.)

Cross — Click on the "cross" icon to delete any parts you've chosen from the drawers, such as shapes and accessories. Highlight, then click on the X.

Page — Click on the "page" icon to delete a whole page. When you finish one project and start the next, you also have to delete the images left on the pasteboard.

Print — Click on the "printer" icon to print your work at any stage. If your project is slow in printing, quit the program to speed it up.

Save — You can save your work at any time by clicking on the "disk" icon. Give your file a name when you save it, and choose somewhere suitable to put it, such as your desktop.

To **resave** it, click on the icon again. You will have to retype your file name to save it again. An alert box will then pop up, asking you whether you wish to replace the original. Click "Yes" if you have a PC, and "Replace" if you have a Macintosh®.

Open — Open a file by clicking on the "open file" icon. Create a folder to save it in, and you can put as many documents as you like.

The Toolkit

The five drawers contain all you need to create a fantastic plane, which you will then cut and fold to make it three-dimensional. When starting out, it's easiest to work through these drawers roughly in the order shown below. Remember, you must close one drawer before you can open another.

Template

1. Open the "Templates" drawer to see pictures of all the models. The numbers to the left of each picture refer to the number of templates required to make up each model.

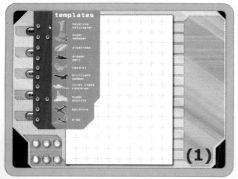

(1)

2. Choose a design that you like, and click on the numbered buttons to fill the screen with that template. Close the drawer.

(2)

Details

The shading on the template represents the parts of the plane that are visible when the model is folded up.

1. Open the "Details" drawer, and a grid will appear, displaying all the designs you can choose from. On the top of the grid, you will be able to see which page you are on, and how many designs there are in total.

To view the next page, click on the right-hand arrow. To view the previous page, click on the left-hand arrow.

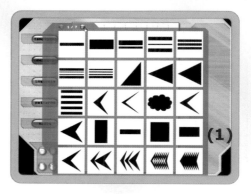

(1)

2. Now for the fun part! Click on the items that you need, and they will appear on the pasteboard. The grid overlay is designed to help you place details onto the gray areas as precisely as possible.

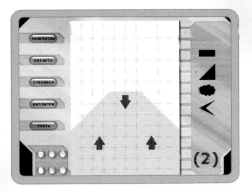

3. Simply drag the item from the pasteboard and toward the gray area. The center of the item will "snap" to the lines present on the grid. You can, of course, place items anywhere outside the gray area, and the grid system will still work. Just remember that these details may be hidden by your folds later. Have fun experimenting!

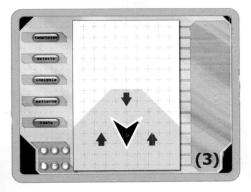

Insignia

The "Insignia" drawer contains loads of cool signs and symbols that you can place anywhere on the template to personalize your plane.

1. To select, simply open the drawer, click on the insignia you want, and it will appear on the pasteboard.

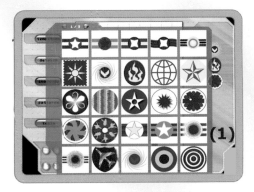

2. Close the drawer, and then experiment where you want to place the image by dragging it over the template, then releasing.

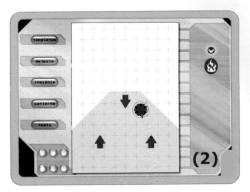

Patterns

Does the template look a bit boring? Well, don't worry, You can change the entire background color!

1. Simply click on any gray part of the template and open the "Patterns" drawer. You'll see lots of different patterns on a grid.

If you like camouflage, or any other pattern, simply click on it.

If you want to make it a plain color, you need to make the background black first, so click on the black square.

2. When you close the drawer, you'll find that the template has filled with your chosen color! Cool!

Remember, if you don't like the pattern you've chosen, simply re-open the "Patterns" drawer, and click on another box in the grid.

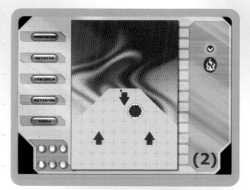

(2)

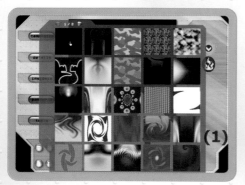

(1)

Tools

This drawer contains two main functions. When you open it, you'll see the buttons that change your images and the "color mixer." Here's what they can do:

Images

You can alter the size and position of images chosen from the "Details" and "Insignia" drawers.

1. Making images larger and smaller

Highlight the image, and click on either the + or the − buttons until it is the required size. You can click on the opposite button if the image gets too large or too small!

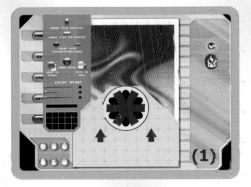
(1)

2. Flipping images around

Highlight the image, and click on the vertical button to turn it upside down, or the horizontal button to switch it to either side.

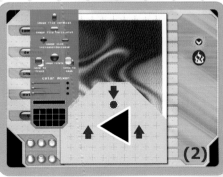
(2)

3. Layering images

If you drag an image from the pasteboard onto the template and then drop another over it, the first will always be behind the other.

If you want to reverse the image order, simply click on the "send to front" icon, and it will bring the first image to the front. To change it back, simply click the "send to back" icon.

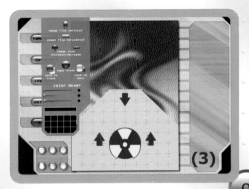
(3)

4. Rotate images

When you drag your item from the pasteboard, it may not be at the correct angle. This tool allows you to rotate items to fit within the dotted gray areas of the template.

Drag the item onto the template itself, click to highlight, and then click on the red "image rotate" icon. This will turn your item 15 degrees with each click of the mouse.

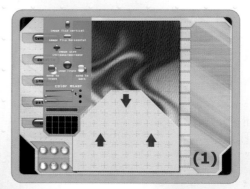

(4)

The Color Palette

This great tool allows you to change the color of your background and plane details with no fuss!

Color Mixer

1. Light and Dark

Open the "Tools" drawer, and you'll see three horizontal lines, with blue circles to the left-hand side of each. Click on a circle, and when a "hand" icon appears, drag it slowly to the right, and you'll see the color getting lighter in the circle on the right-hand side of the line.

(1)

2. Fixing the Color

When you're happy with the color, release the mouse, and double-click on

(2)

the rectangle below. Magic! The color is stored in the grid-style palette. Keep going until you have all the colors you need.

You can mix any color of your choice by combining two or three color bars. You will need to determine which colors must be combined to make the color you want. Yellow is made from red and green, so drag one bar to red, another to green and yellow will appear in the rectangle. Double click on the rectangle to save the new color in the palette. You can put 15 colors in the palette.

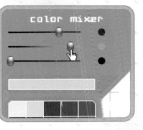

Using the Colors

You can change the color of anything that is plain black. This includes the background and any black images selected from the "Details" drawer.

1. Background
(A) To change the background to one plain color, you need to go to the "Patterns"  drawer and select the black square from the grid. Close this drawer, click on the background to highlight it, and then open the "Tools" drawer.

(B) Selecting any color you've mixed in your palette will change the background to  the shade of your choice. Close the drawer to get the full effect! You can only change the color of the solid black background, not the color of patterned backgrounds.

2. Details
(A) To change any black images from the "Details" drawer, simply click on the part you 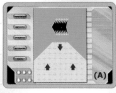 want to change to highlight it.

(B) Open the "Tools" drawer and click on a color of your choice from the palette. Close the 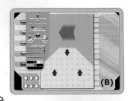 drawer. Of course, you can change the color if you are unsure simply by highlighting the image and repeating this process.

3. Printing
Once you are happy with the overall look of your template, save again and click on the "printer" icon in the bottom left-hand corner of the studio. Once your template has printed out, cut around the black outline, and it's ready to go!

11

Hovering Helicopter

⚠ You will need:

- a completed Hovering Helicopter template
- scissors

1. Cut along all the solid lines marked on your template.

2. Fold flap A forward, and flap B to the back.

3. Fold both flaps C and D forward along the dotted lines. (Fold the entire length of the template, including part E.)

4. Fold along the horizontal line E, and then fold the flap upwards to add some weight to the helicopter.

5. Make sure the blades are folded horizontally to each other, and then drop the helicopter from a height (such as from the top of the stairs). It will stay in the air for a long time, spiraling quickly as it comes down.

F Helicopter Facts

Did you know?

◎ *Even if a helicopter's engine cuts out, the blades continue to spin, which means it still has a chance of a safe landing.*

◎ *U.S. police and emergency rescue helicopters help about 15,000 people a year.*

◎ *The first rescue operation was in 1944, when a helicopter lifted someone from the sea.*

◎ *Helicopters are very fast. The current world helicopter speed record is held by the Westland Lynx, which can travel at 250 mph (402 km/h).*

Super Swooper

! You will need:

- completed Super Swooper plane templates

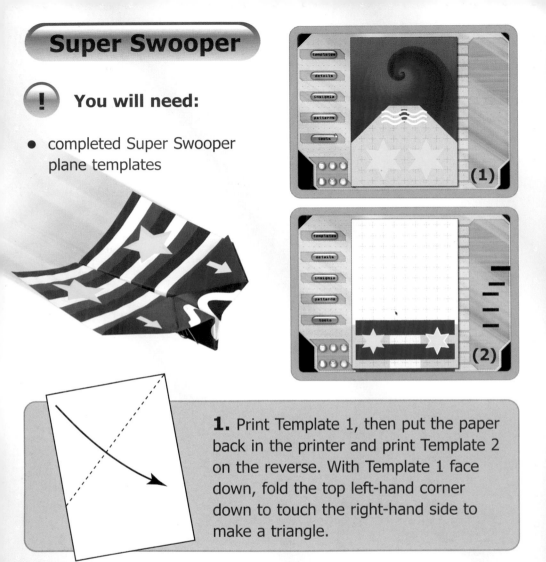

(1)

(2)

1. Print Template 1, then put the paper back in the printer and print Template 2 on the reverse. With Template 1 face down, fold the top left-hand corner down to touch the right-hand side to make a triangle.

2. Fold the top point of the model down to reach the bottom-left hand side of the triangle. You should now have a house-shaped model, made from a rectangle with a triangle on the top.

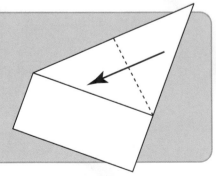

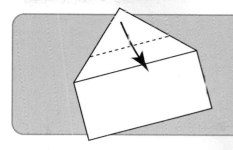

3. Fold the top point of the triangle down to reach one-third of the way up the rectangle below it.

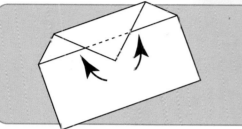

4. Fold the overlapping tip of the triangle under the flap beneath it.

5. Fold the model in half from left to right.

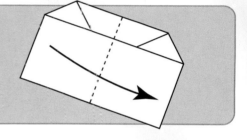

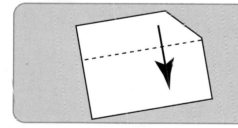

6. Fold down each side of the model to form the wings.

 Flying Tip!

Hold the Super Swooper just under the nose, and throw overhand with a slight upward push.

Albatross

 You will need:

- a completed Albatross template

1. Place the template colored side down. Fold the template in half vertically from left to right and then unfold it leaving a crease.

2. Fold the bottom left-hand corner about two-thirds across, as shown.

3. Repeat Step 2 with the right-hand corner, as shown, leaving a slight triangle to overlap the model.

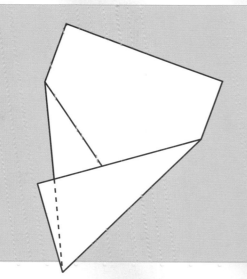

4. Turn the plane over, and fold the nose upward to lie along the dotted line, as shown.

5. Fold and unfold along the center line, and then make two vertical creases about 4/5 inch (2 cm) away from each side of it, as shown.

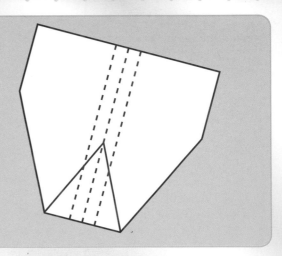

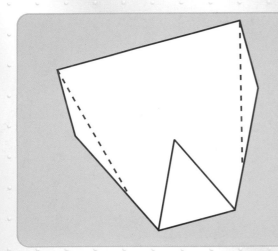

6. Make folds at the end of each wing, as shown. Make sure that they fold downward or the plane will fly upside down!

 **Glider Facts**

Did you know?

◎ *This plane is based on a glider. The earliest planes were of this type and were being built in the late 1700s. They are a heavier-than-air craft without an engine.*

◎ *George Cayley built the first glider in 1799 and flew it in 1804. He inspired many people, including Otto Lilienthal, who appeared in many newspapers when he and his glider floated gracefully over the hillsides. It was the first time that people had ever seen someone flying—even if it wasn't for long.*

◎ *Tragedy struck when he and his glider crashed from 50 feet (15 m) in 1896. Lilienthal's work, however, was very important because it became the basis of what we know about flying planes today.*

✈ Flying Tip!

● This plane flies best in a non-turbulent environment. The slightest gust of wind will make it crash, so have fun indoors!

● Hold the plane 2 inches (5 cm) from the nose, point slightly upward, and give it a gentle overhand throw.

Remember: Practice makes perfect. If you throw this plane too hard, it will spiral out of control and crash. Easy does it!

19

Dragon Dart

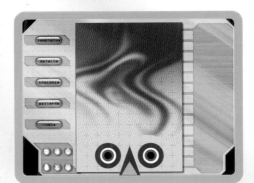

 You will need:

- a completed Dragon Dart template

1. Place the template colored side down. Fold and unfold the template vertically, from left to right.

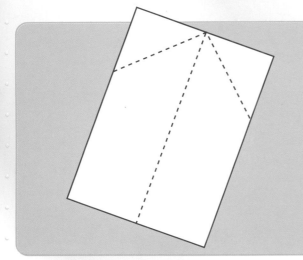

2. Fold the top left- and right-hand corners to the central crease.

3. Fold the top left and right edges to lie along the central crease, along the dotted lines shown.

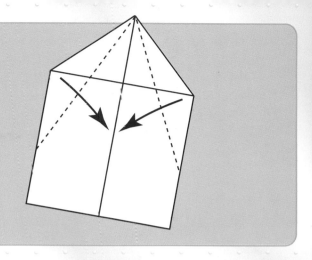

4. Fold the top point of the model downward to lie along the dotted line, as shown.

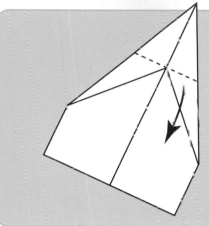

5. Fold the top right and left corners along the diagonal dotted lines, as shown, to meet the central crease.

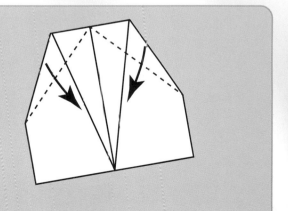

6. Fold the downward-facing triangular flap upward so that its tip touches the top of the model. It is very important that the tip meets the top point as neatly as possible.

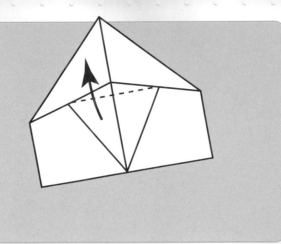

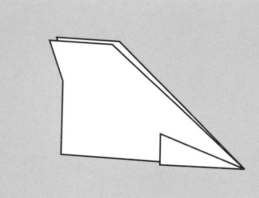

7. Fold the model in half. The side view should look like this!

8. To make the wings, fold along the dotted lines shown in the diagram.

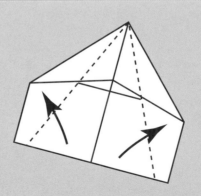

 **Flying Tip!**

- Hold the plane around 2 inches (5 cm) from the tip and throw it hard, overhand.
- You can make a back tail fin by pushing the back end of the model upward and into a point.

 F **Fighter Trivia**

◎ *This model is based on a fighter plane. Take a look at some of the great fighters that have been built throughout the years. How many have you heard of?*

P-51 Mustangs

◎ **1930s:** *Supermarine Spitfire, P-38 Lightning*

◎ **1940s:** *P-47 Thunderbolt, P-51 Mustang*

◎ **1950s:** *F-80 Shooting Star, F-86 Sabre*

F-4 Phantom

◎ **1960s:** *F-104 Starfighter, F-105 Thunderchief*

◎ **1970s:** *F-4 Phantom, A-4 Skyhawk*

◎ **1980s:** *F-15 Eagle, F-16 Falcon*

F-16 Falcon

◎ **1990s:** *F-117 Nighthawk, MiG-31 Foxhound*

Eurofighter

◎ **2000s:** *F-22 Raptor, Eurofighter*

Kestrel

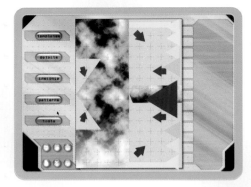

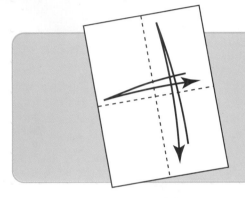

1. Place your template colored side down, triangles to the left. Fold the opposite edges together in turn, press flat and open up.

2. Fold the left-hand corners over, as shown.

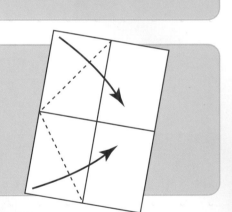

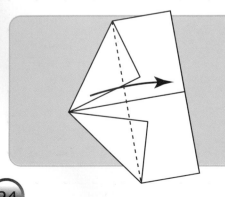

3. Fold the left-hand point over to meet the middle of the opposite side.

24

4. Again, fold the left-hand corners over.

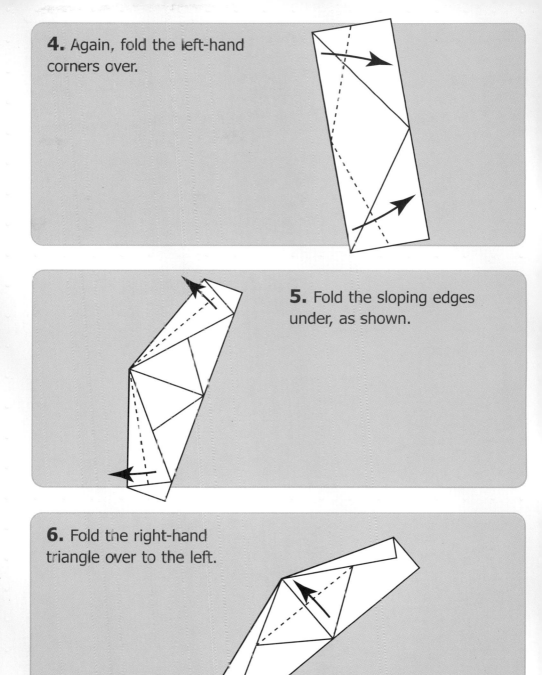

5. Fold the sloping edges under, as shown.

6. Fold the right-hand triangle over to the left.

25

7. Fold the bottom edge behind to meet the top edge.

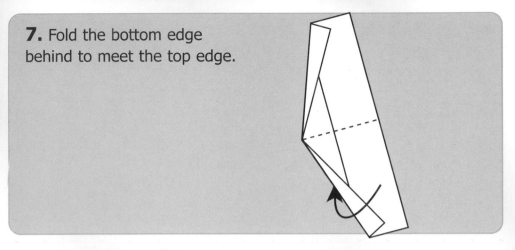

8. Fold the front flap forward and the back flap behind, making the wings.

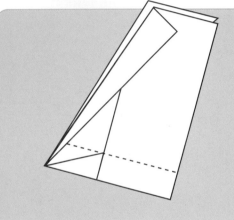

9. Fold the front wing up. Repeat behind.

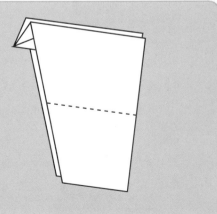

10. Fold a little of the front wing's top edge behind. Repeat with the back wing.

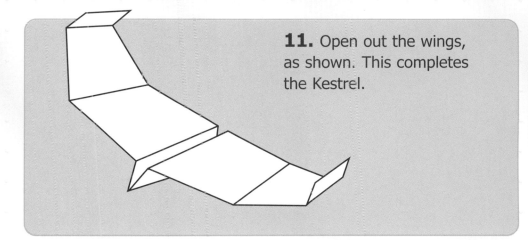

11. Open out the wings, as shown. This completes the Kestrel.

 Flying Tip!

● Throw high up, fairly gently, and watch the Kestrel float gracefully downward.

Brilliant Bomber

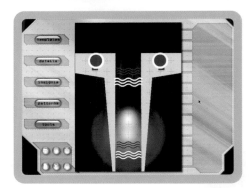

 You will need:

- a completed Brilliant Bomber template
- a pair of scissors
- a paper clip

1. Make three folds across the template, as shown, using the dotted lines as a guide.

2. Fold the template in half from top to bottom, and cut away a section as indicated by the cutting marks on the template.

3. Fold down the wings, in the position indicated by the dotted lines on the template. Add a paper clip onto the nose, and it's ready to fly!

F Bomber Facts

One of the most famous bombers of all time is the B-17 Flying Fortress. Check out these heavyweight facts!

B-17 Flying Fortress

◎ *Wingspan: 104 ft. (32 m)*
◎ *Weight: up to 55,000 lbs loaded (25,000 kilograms)*

◎ *Range: up to 1,850 miles (3,420 kilometers)*
◎ *Top speed: 300 mph (555 km/h)*

✈ Flying Tip!

• Change the depth, angle, and size of the cut in Step 2 to increase the number of tricks your bomber is able to perform.

1st-Class Concorde

! You will need:

- a completed Concorde template
- a piece of card
- glue
- scissors
- sticky putty

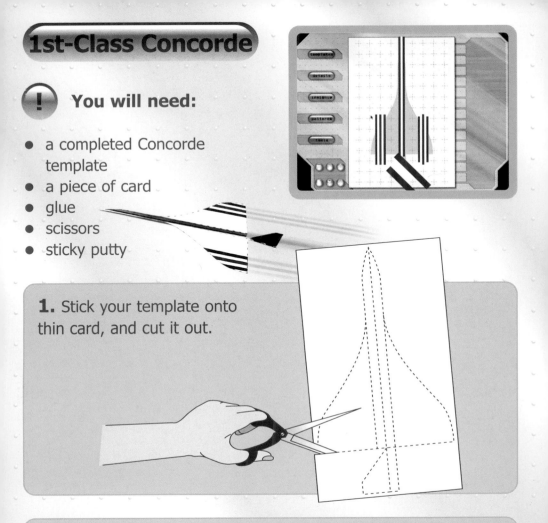

1. Stick your template onto thin card, and cut it out.

2. Fold the plane in half so that the wings point upward. Make sure that the wings are the same size. Planes with uneven wings will crash!

3. Stick your template onto thin card, and cut it out.

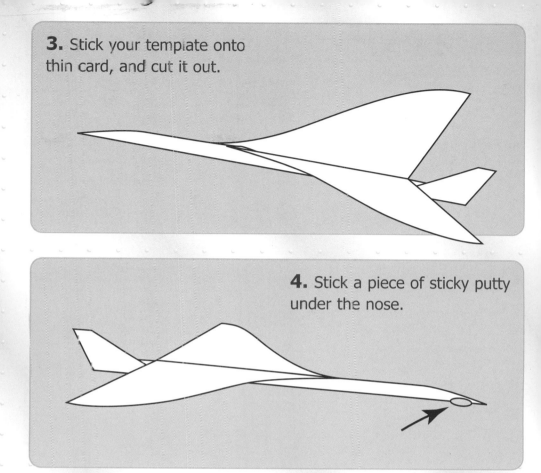

4. Stick a piece of sticky putty under the nose.

F Concorde Trivia

◎ *Concorde is the fastest passenger plane in the world. It travels at 1,340 mph (2,150 km/h)—twice the speed of sound!*

◎ *Length: 204 ft (63 m)*

◎ *Wingspan: 83 ft 8 inches (25 m)*

◎ *Concorde's speed means that it can leave London in the afternoon and arrive in New York earlier the same day!*

✈ Flying Tip!

● Hold your Concorde between your thumb and forefinger, in front of the wings. Hold it above your shoulder and throw hard, with the front slightly raised.

Super Shuttle

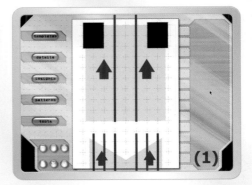

(1)

! You will need:

- a sheet of letter paper
- two completed Super Shuttle templates
- scissors
- tape
- two paper clips

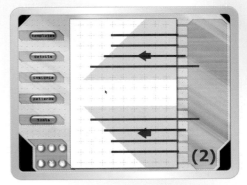

(2)

1. Roll the piece of paper to make a cylinder with a diameter of 2 inches (5 cm). Use tape to hold it together.

2. Fold Template 1 in half from left to right along the dotted lines indicated on the template. Then fold the left and right-hand corners to the center fold.

3. Tape the assembled cylinder onto Template 1. This forms the body and wings of the Space Shuttle.

4. Cut the rectangle from Template 2, and fold it in half along the dotted line. Then fold up the tabs at both ends.

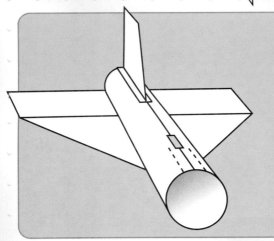

5. Cut a fin shape along the cutting lines of the template, and stick it to the back of the cylinder.

6. Cut slots measuring 1 3/4 inches (4 cm) along the nose end of the cylinder. Fold down the resulting flap to form the cockpit.

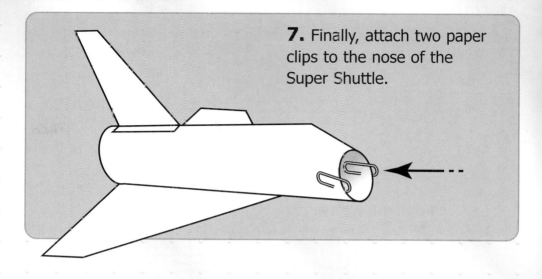

7. Finally, attach two paper clips to the nose of the Super Shuttle.

 **Lift-Off!**

A shuttle needs the four following things to lift it into orbit:

◎ *Two solid rocket boosters (These provide 71 percent of the upward thrust.)*

◎ *Three main engines (each 14 ft, or 4 m, long, providing the remaining 29 percent of the thrust)*

◎ *External fuel tank (158 ft or 48 m long, holding huge amounts of propellant)*

◎ *Orbital maneuvering system (which guides shuttle into, between, and back into orbit).*

 **Flying Tip!**

● To launch your Super Shuttle, gently grip it at the back, hold it in front of your shoulder, and throw forward with the front raised.

Throwing Technique

Over the next few pages, you will see how to make tiny replicas of two very famous planes by customizing the several templates that make each 3-D model.

You simply have to print them onto thin card, cut around the shapes, and put them together. Although it may seem hard to believe, these minifliers work on exactly the same principles as a jumbo jet or fighter plane!

Just like an airplane, the wings on your miniflier are a special aerodynamic shape. In most cases, the wing is curved on top, so that air travels faster over it. As a result, the air pressure above the wing is reduced. This creates a small vacuum, and the airplane gets sucked up into the air!

Perfect Grip

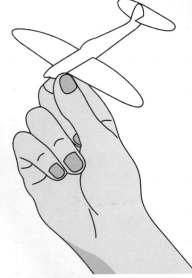

Using your thumb and forefinger, grip the miniflier on the bottom near the front.

If you want to become an ace pilot, you'll need to perfect a really good throwing technique. The following top tips will enable you to control the performance of your minifliers. Get ready for takeoff!

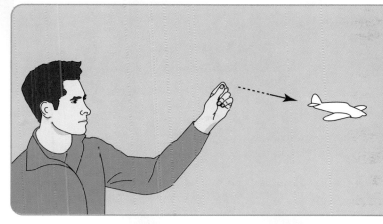

Slow Flight

Hold the plane in front of your shoulder. Throw gently forward, with the front slightly lowered.

Fast Flight

Hold the plane above your shoulder. Throw hard, with the front slightly raised.

High Flight

Hold the plane above your shoulder. Throw hard, with the front pointing toward the sky.

 Remember:

Practice makes perfect! Don't give up if your first throw is more of a flop than a flight!

The Spitfire was the most important airplane on the Allied side in Europe in World War II. Its main opponent was the German Messerschmitt Bf 109. The Spitfire's markings made it a very distinctive airplane.

Supermarine Spitfire

Many versions of the Spitfire were made. Their general outline remained the same, but they were upgraded many times, and very few fit a single description.

You can base your designs on some of the following Spitfire models. If you like, you can research these models to see exactly what they looked like.

Model	Number Produced	Did You Know?
Mark 1	1,569	*This was unpopular with pilots because the cannons often jammed!*
Mark IV	229	*This had an extra torsion box to hold more fuel.*
Mark V	6,478	*This had an air filter to keep the sand out when flying in deserts.*
Mark VIII	1,653	*This was modified for tropical conditions.*
Mark IX	7,180	*The most successful model, this used a new version of the original Merlin engine.*

Putting Together Your Spitfire Model

(!) **You will need:**

- a completed Spitfire template
- scissors

1. Design your templates on the page, using the images, patterns, and text from the CD. Print them out onto thin card.

2. Make small cuts along the dotted lines shown on the templates.

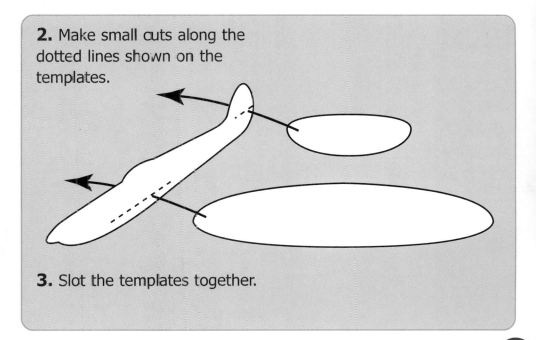

3. Slot the templates together.

B-52 Replica

The B-52 Stratofortress is probably the most important plane in the U.S. Air Force.

It made its first flight in 1954, and its technology has been updated ever since then.

What makes it such a special airplane?

- It can drop a wide array of weapons (bombs and guided missiles).

- The "H" model can carry up to 20 air-launched cruise missiles.

- It can refuel in mid-air.

- It has a combat (fighting) range of more than 8,750 miles (14,080 km). It can go this far without refueling!

- It can fly at subsonic speeds at altitudes of 50,000 feet!

Boeing B-52 Stratofortress

 **B-52 Facts**

- *Main function: Heavy long-range bomber*

- *Length: 159 feet, 4 inches (48.5 m)*

- *Height: 40 feet, 8 inches (12.5 m)*

- *Wingspan: 185 feet (56 m)*

- *Speed: 650 mph (1,046 km/h)*

Putting Together Your B-52 Model

 You will need:

- a completed B-52 template
- scissors

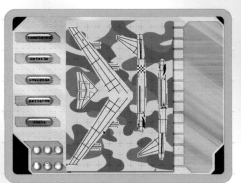

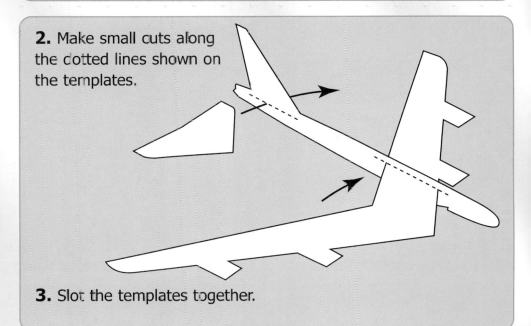

1. Design your templates on the page, using the images, patterns, and text from the CD. Print them out onto thin card.

2. Make small cuts along the dotted lines shown on the templates.

3. Slot the templates together.

Record Breakers

These aircraft are all world-record breakers!

First Powered Flight

The Wright brothers' first flight on Dec. 17, 1903, was just a hop at 12 seconds.

Smallest Plane

The Sky Baby is the plane with the world's shortest wingspan—just 5 feet (1.67 m) long!

Largest Wingspan

The Hughes Hercules flying boat (also known as the Spruce Goose) only completed one test run—but it had a wingspan of 320 feet (97 m) long.

Super Speedy

The U.S. Air Force Lockheed SR-71 was the fastest jet ever, reaching 2,193 mph (3,530 km/h)!

The Biggest Carrier

The Airbus A380 is designed to carry more than 800 people!

The World's Best Paper Pilot!

You may never get a chance to be an airplane pilot or a space shuttle astronaut. However, with this book and CD, you can try as many times as you like to become the world's best paper pilot! A scoresheet at the back of this book, on page 48, lets you chart all your flying attempts. Here are the records to beat!

 Paper Plane Facts

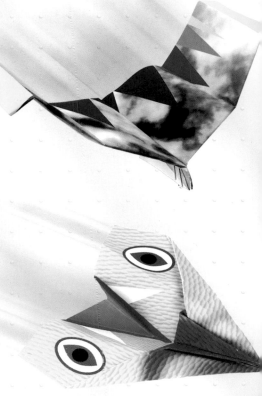

◎ *The longest recorded distance a paper airplane has flown is 193.01 ft (58 m).*

◎ *The world record for paper airplane time aloft (length of time your plane stays in the air) is 27.6 seconds!*

◎ *The largest paper airplane on record had a wingspan that measured 45.01 ft (13 m) across!*

◎ *The smallest paper airplane on record was made from a piece of paper that measured about 3/8 by 1/4 inch (0.4 by 0.6 cm), about the length and width of a single staple!*

Pictorial Index

Details Insignia Patterns

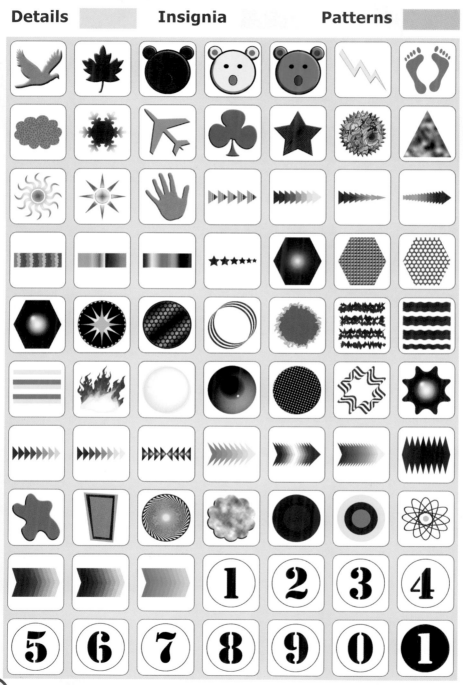

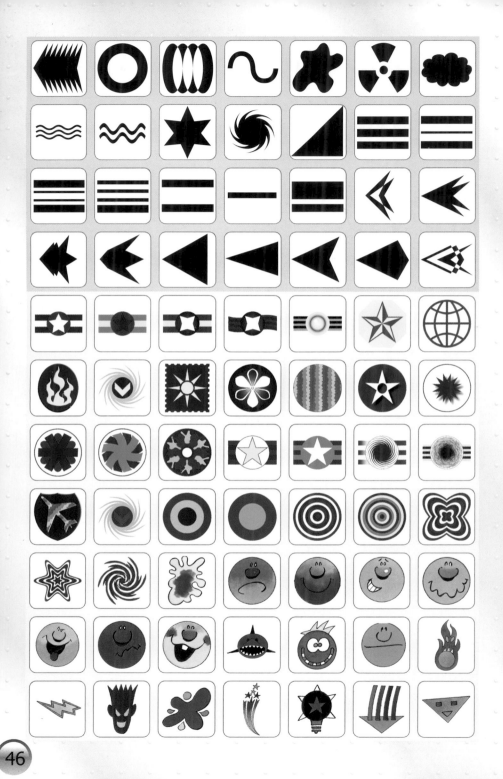

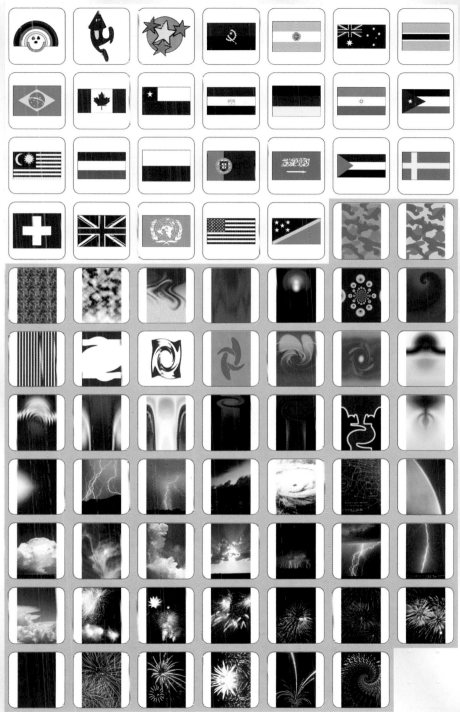

Flight Record

Name of flier	Distance thrown	Time in air flight	Conditions	Date